Mollebakken

Mollebakken

The Rise of Bloodaxe

Eric Schumacher

Copyright (C) 2019 Eric Schumacher
Layout design and Copyright (C) 2019 by Next Chapter
Published 2019 by Next Chapter
Cover art: David Brzozowski, BlueSpark Studios
(additional art by Andrew Dodor and Dominik Mayer)
Back cover texture by David M. Schrader, used under license from Shutterstock.com
Large Print Edition
All rights reserved. No part of this book may be reproduced or transmitted in any form or by any means, electronic or mechanical, including photocopying, recording, or by any information storage and retrieval system, without the author's permission.

To my family and friends, for your love, your patience, and your continued support.

Acknowledgements

There are many people to thank for the creation of this novella. First and foremost, to my publisher, Next Chapter, and those authors who urged me to tell Hakon's backstory – I thank you for pushing me to pursue this idea. I again bow in thanks to the keen eyes and attention to detail of Marg Gilks and Lori Weathers, who honed my words into the story you are about to read. With each book, I endeavor to present a cover that helps set the tone and vision for the story. Thankfully, I have masters like David Brzozowski for layout, and Dominik Mayer and Andrew Dodor for imagery, to transform my ideas into a work of art. And last but certainly not least, I want to thank you, my readers, for your continued support, your nudges, your reviews of my work, your comments on social media, and for so much more. It is to you all, and to the countless others who have accompanied me on this journey, that I owe a huge debt of gratitude.

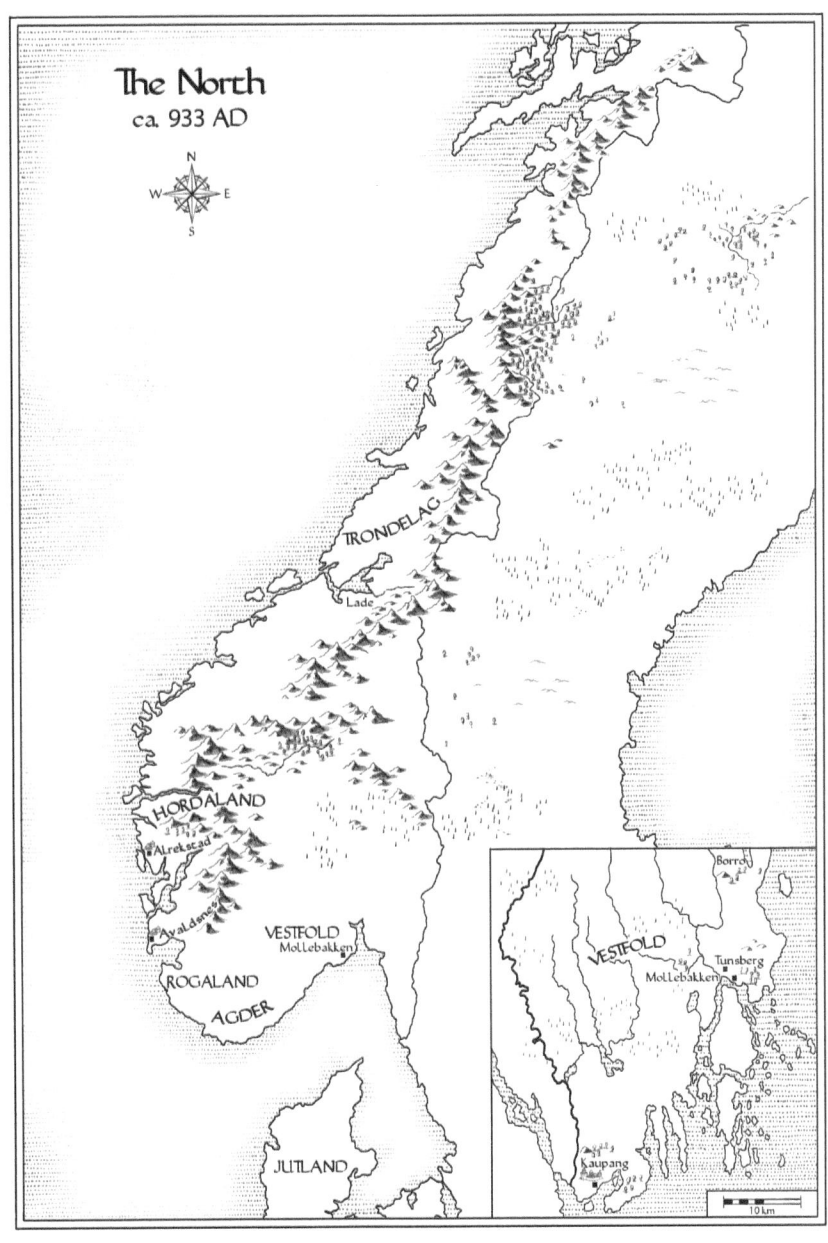

Glossary

Aesir – One of the main tribes of deities venerated by the pre-Christian Norse. Old Norse: *Æsir*.
Balder – One of the Aesir gods. He is often associated with love, peace, justice, purity, and poetry. Old Norse: *Baldr*.
bonder – Free men (farmers, craftsmen, etc.) who enjoyed rights such as the use of weapons and the right to attend law-things. They constituted the middle class. Old Norse: *baendr*.
byrnie – A (usually short-sleeved) chain mail shirt that hung to the upper thigh. Old Norse: *brynja*.
dragon – A larger class of Viking warship. Old Norse: *Dreki*.
Dubhlinn Norse – Northmen who live in Dublin.
Eastern Sea – Baltic Sea.
Frey – Brother to the goddess Freya. He is often associated with virility and prosperity, with sunshine and fair weather. Old Norse: *Freyr*.

Freya – Sister to god Frey. She is often associated with love, sex, beauty, fertility, gold, magic, war, and death. Old Norse: *Freyja*.

Frigga – he is the highest-ranking of the Aesir goddesses. She's the wife of Odin, the leader of the gods, and the mother of the god Baldur. She is often confused with Freya. Old Norse: *Frigg*.

fylke (pl. **fylker**) – Old Norse for "folkland," which has come to mean "county" in modern use.

godi – A heathen priest or chieftain. Old Norse: *goði*.

hird – A personal retinue of armed companions who formed the nucleus of a household guard. Hird means "household." Old Norse *hirð*.

hirdman (pl. **hirdmen**) – A member or members of the hird. Old Norse: *hirðman*.

hlaut – The blood of sacrificed animals.

Holmgard – The Old Norse name for Novgorod.

Irland – Ireland.

Island – Iceland.

jarl – Old Norse for "earl."

jarldom – The area of land that a jarl ruled.

kaupang – Old Norse for "marketplace." It is also the name of the main market town in Norway that existed around AD 800–950.

knarr – A type of merchant ship. Old Norse: *knǫrr*.

Midgard – The Norse name for Earth and the place inhabited by humans. Old Norse: *Miðgarðr*.

Night Mare – The Night Mare is an evil spirit that rides on people's chests while they sleep, bringing bad dreams. Old Norse: *Mara*.

Njord – A god associated with sea, seafaring, wind, fishing, wealth, and crop fertility. Old Norse: *Njörðr*.

Norns – The three female divine beings who influence the course of a man's destiny. Their names are Urd (Old Norse *Urðr*, "What Once Was"), Verdandi (Old Norse *Verðandi*, "What Is Coming into Being"), and Skuld (Old Norse *Skuld*, "What Shall Be").

Odin – Husband to Frigga. The god associated with healing, death, royalty, knowledge, battle, and sorcery. He oversees Valhall, the hall of the slain. Old Norse: *Óðinn*.

Orkneyjar – The Orkney Islands.

seax – A knife or short sword. Also known as scramaseax, or wounding knife.

Sjaelland – The largest Danish island.

sjaund – A ritual drinking feast held seven days after a death to celebrate the life of the person and to officially pass that person's inheritance on to his or her next of kin.

skald – A poet. Old Norse: *skald* or *skáld*.

shield wall – A shield wall was a "wall of shields" formed by warriors standing in formation shoulder to shoulder, holding their shields so that they abut or overlap. Old Norse: *skjaldborg*.

steer board – A rudder affixed to the right stern of a ship. The origin of the word "starboard." Old Norse: *stýri* (rudder) and *borð* (side of the ship).

skeid – A midsize class of Viking warship.

skol – A toast to others when drinking. Old Norse: *skál*.

thing – The governing assembly of a Viking society or region, made up of the free people of the community and presided over by lawspeakers. Old Norse: *þing*.

Thor – A hammer-wielding god associated with thunder, lightning, storms, oak trees, strength, and the protection of mankind. Old Norse: *Þórr*.

thrall – A slave.

Valhall (also **Valhalla**) – The hall of the slain presided over by Odin. It is where brave warriors chosen by valkyries go when they die. Old Norse: *Valhöll*.

valkyrie – A female helping spirit of Odin that transports his favorite among those slain in battle to Valhall, where they will fight by his side during the battle at the end of time, Ragnarok. Old Norse: *valkyrja* (pl. *valkyrjur*).

wergeld – Also known as "man price," it was the value placed on every being and piece of property.

woolsark – A shirt or vest made of coarse wool.

Yngling – Refers to the Fairhair dynasty, who descended from the kings of Uplands, Norway, and who trace their lineage back to the god Frey.

Foreword

Long ago, when I began writing the story of Hakon the Good, I also began exploring other people and events to which he owed his rise in tenth century Norway. This novella tells the story of a specific event — a battle that occurred circa AD 933 — that paved the way for Hakon's return from England soon after. Though it is barely mentioned in Snorri Sturlason's *Heimskringla*, I have come to believe that the battle of Mollebakken (as I am calling it) is one of the more consequential battles of the Viking Age.

Chapter 1

Avaldsnes, Norway. November, AD 930

The winter sky had lightened to the color of ash by the time Erik navigated his ship into the bay below his father's great estate at Avaldsnes. Erik tightened the woolen cloak around his chest to warm himself, then surveyed the landscape with gray-green eyes moist from the cold. Though the sun was up, torches lit Harald's estate and cast the entire area in an eerie glow that shifted and stirred like a vision from a strange dream.

"It is quiet." The comment from Erik's foster brother, Arinbjorn, put voice to Erik's thoughts. Only four sentries stood on the beach and their stillness put Erik in mind of boulders, not men. The only other sign of life came from the occasional call of a lone seagull roaming the fjord.

"Aye," he answered as his gaze shifted from one sentry to the next.

Erik's ship glided forward, bobbing in the gentle waves. On the strand, one of the sentries moved off in the direction of the great hall looming on the hill at the south end of the beach. Erik could see a cluster of men gathering there, but did not see his father among them.

As soon as the ship ground to a halt on the pebbles, Erik vaulted the gunwale and splashed into the shallow surf. Arinbjorn and ten of Erik's most trusted hirdmen followed. "What news of my father?" Erik asked the approaching sentries by way of greeting.

"He is at his hall, lord, and is expecting you."

The sentries led Erik and his men from the beach toward the group of men gathered near the great hall. It was as they climbed the trail that Erik saw his father. Though surrounded by his hirdmen and advisors, Harald's hulking shoulders and shock of white hair were unmistakable. Erik would have smiled, but the faces of Harald's councilors made him frown. The councilors were Harald's most trusted men — advisors and wealthy bonders who attended him when matters of import required their presence. Normally they came to Harald between spring and autumn, or met with the king at the law assembly in high summer. It was uncommon to see them here, in the winter.

"What are the councilors doing here?" he huffed to Arinbjorn. "They should be home for winter."

Arinbjorn could only shrug.

As Erik reached the group, the councilors bowed and stepped back to let Erik pass, revealing a man Erik barely recognized. Though still taller than many of his men, Harald's body had hunched and softened dramatically. The hair that had once earned him the byname of Fairhair clung to his head in thin, stringy wisps of white. Above pink bags of flesh that rested on his jowls, Harald's blue eyes were now sunken and misted with age. He grinned through his beard and reached out to his son with fingers that looked like the branches of some long-dead tree.

They embraced, then parted, and Harald held his son at arm's length to gaze into his eyes. "You are surprised to see me like this." His voice wavered with age.

Erik looked down, angry at himself for not suppressing his alarm and embarrassed that his father had detected it so easily.

Harald barked a short laugh and patted his shoulder. "What did you believe you would find?

A young man? Hah. Age takes its toll on every man, especially when you have lived as long and as hard as me. But enough of this. You remember my councilors, do you not?" Harald swept his arm theatrically toward them.

Erik smiled politely to them, though nothing in him felt like being polite. "I do."

Harald grunted and grabbed his son's arm. "Come. Let us go inside and find some warmth. My old bones do not like the cold."

The journey into the great hall took longer than Erik expected. Weight had so weakened Harald's knees that the old man needed someone on each arm to support him, and even then, he paused every ten steps for breath. He grunted and snorted, and his sagging cheeks turned a deep crimson with the effort. Yet, in his obstinacy, he refused to sit until he had walked the length of his hall — more than one hundred paces.

Halfway across the hall, Erik glanced at Arinbjorn. The other man pursed his lips and shook his head sadly. Erik turned away, disgusted by the frailty that had overcome his father. Here was a man who, through unnatural intelligence, incredible strength, and unyielding will, had conquered the whole of the North — the first king ever to accomplish such a task. A legend not only in his own land, but throughout Midgard. A man that Erik had tried hard to emulate. And yet, this same man, this godlike being, could now barely walk from one end of his hall to the other. Erik forced himself to focus on other things, lest he lose control of his temper, but his thoughts would not unbind, and by the time they reached the opposite end of the hall, he had worked himself into a frenzy of frustration.

Harald sat heavily in the High Seat of Norway — a massive oak chair carved with the interweaving, serpentine pattern so commonly found in the art of the day. Its massive arms ended in dragon claws, which Harald gripped as he pushed his girth farther back onto the High Seat. Two thralls appeared then with a pine table and placed it before the king. On the opposite side of the table they placed a short bench.

Harald motioned to his councilors. "Leave us. You also, Arinbjorn." He then turned his crimson face to Erik. "Please. Sit." He motioned to the bench. "We have much to discuss."

As Erik sat, a pretty serving girl brought a pitcher of red glass and filled two silver drinking cups. Harald let his eyes linger on the girl as she poured.

"I see your appreciation for beautiful women has not abated," commented Erik. The girl's cheeks turned as red as the pitcher in her hand.

Harald grinned. "As you know, I have always had a weakness for women. When I was young, it was about the chase and, of course, the conquest. Why do you think I have so many children, eh?" He barked a laugh, then quickly sobered. "But times change. Now they are the only thing that keeps this old heart pumping." He tapped his thick chest as the serving girl moved away. "But enough of that." Harald lifted his horn with a shaking hand. "A toast. To your future."

"And to yours," Erik responded lamely, unable to think of anything else to say.

Harald snorted. "My future has long past, Erik. But I accept your toast nonetheless."

They drank deeply from their cups and Erik smacked his lips in appreciation. After several days on the sea, it was a pleasure to feel the wine work its warmth in his gut.

Harald smiled and the lines around his eyes creased deeply. "Tell me, how fares your family?"

"They are well. Gunnhild has produced another son, whom we have named Harald. If his body grows as strong as his lungs, then he should have no problem in this world. The other lads are fine, too. As you know, Beard-Thorir now fosters Ragnvald, who is entering his twelfth winter. He is a good boy. Strong and well-spoken. I have high hopes for him."

Harald took another lingering draught, then replaced his cup on the arm of his chair. "He is nearly marrying age."

"Aye, and I have my eyes on a few who might suit us well."

Harald's left brow rose. "Anyone I know?"

"Most certainly. Groa Ivarsdottir of the Uplands and Kara Hervardssdottir from Halogaland. Either would do, though I would prefer Groa."

Harald twined his gnarled fingers together and brought them to his lips. It was a gesture he used when thinking and one, Erik had learned, that permitted no interruptions. After a moment, Harald nodded. "Aye. I believe you are right in that. Groa would do quite well. We have never been very friendly with the Uplanders and there would be much to gain from such a union. What of Gunnhild? How does she fare?"

"Still as strong in mind as ever. A woman to be reckoned with."

Harald grinned. "I would expect that. The moment that woman submits to your will is the moment you should start worrying for her health."

A thrall placed a few more logs in the large hearth in the center of the hall, then stoked the flames until the wood began to snap and pop. Erik could feel the heat on his back and removed his cloak to enjoy the warmth. Neither father nor son moved to speak, content instead on the presence of the other and the glow of the fire.

Erik took another gulp of mead and sighed — he could abide his curiosity no longer. "Father, your summons sounded urgent, and you have all of your councilors here. Was there something you wished to discuss besides my family?"

Harald grinned again. "You have never been one to dawdle, my son." The old man hefted his cup and took another sip, then slowly placed the vessel on the table. "Very well. I shall tell you plainly. I have decided to abdicate my High Seat."

"You have decided to *what*?"

The edge in Erik's voice caused Harald to gesture for peace. "I am old, Erik. Too old to run a country effectively. I can no longer do most of the tasks required of me as king. I can barely walk across my own hall or pour two cups of wine." He held up his age-gnarled hands as if to prove his statement.

"But... you still have your mind. That is all you need."

"That, too, will go. It already has. I forget names. Memories have faded."

"But father —"

"You know I speak the truth, Erik. I see it in your face. In your eyes. I am getting too old and it is time to step down."

"No," Erik protested.

Harald looked more amused than offended at Erik's outburst. "Do you not want the arvel of inheritance?"

Erik's jaw dropped.

Harald laughed. "Aye. Now you understand."

Erik had known a day like this might come, but he had never expected it to happen this way. He had always assumed his father would fall in battle and that his own ascension to the High Seat would come only after summers of conflict between his brothers. But this? This was too…what? Too easily done? Too simple?

Harald smiled. "I thought you might react this way."

"Forgive me. I am merely startled by the suddenness of it all. Why me? You have other sons."

Harald's eyebrows rose in surprise. "You do not want the High Seat?"

"No, no." Erik shook his head. "That is not what I am saying."

"Do you doubt your ability, then?"

Erik straightened immediately, his chin thrust outward. "No."

Harald studied his son. "Erik, you are the strongest of my sons in will and prowess. Your successes here and abroad have shown me that. You are a bit headstrong, perchance, but that can be a good thing in the right circumstances. You are also the most ruthless — a trait you will need all too often."

Erik's mind was too filled with discordant thoughts to think of an appropriate response. There was something missing here, something he couldn't quite grasp. He lifted his cup and drank deeply of the wine, trying desperately to subdue the troubled feelings that swirled within him. "Do my half-brothers know of your abdication?"

Harald shrugged as if it were of no concern. "They will soon enough."

"You did not invite them here?"

"I did not *want* them here."

"Why?"

"Why should I? I have sent messengers to them with my decision. They may come in time."

"My half-brothers will not accept this news lightly."

"No, they will not," Harald agreed. "But I have taken measures to appease them. They shall keep their lands for now, and a portion of the taxes that will come from those lands. Any attempt on their part to widen their borders or challenge my ruling will be met with force. When I die, things will change, of course. But for now, I believe they will accept this." Harald paused to sip at his wine. "So," he concluded, "do you accept my offer?"

"I would be a fool not to," said Erik, who still felt himself reeling from the suddenness of it all.

"Good. On the morrow, then, we shall host a ceremony and rightfully pass the High Seat to you." Harald lifted his cup once again. "And we will drink then to the new king of the North."

The following morning, the call of Harald's battle horn summoned the men to the great hall. Councilors and warriors and those of Harald's family living on the estate trickled into the cavernous space and settled themselves on the wooden platforms that stretched the length of the hall's two long walls.

Erik stood near the entrance, watching the people enter. As he did, he could not help but feel cheated by the whole event. Here he was, on the threshold of his greatest moment — nay, his greatest victory — and the only people to witness it were those who bowed to him already. What of his family? Did they not deserve to stand by his side and be publicly acknowledged as the heirs to this Seat? What of the other northern chieftains and jarls? Had he not won the right to stand before them all and be avowed as their rightful king? And what of his half-brothers? Oh, to look into their forlorn faces and gloat as they bent to his kingship! But this? This was not how he had dreamed it would be, and that thought ate at him.

"Is everything alright, my lord? You look a bit flushed."

Erik turned his eyes to the chief steward of Harald's household and forced a smile. "I am fine."

The steward smiled grandly. "Well, have no cares. It is a simple affair."

A simple affair. The words stung Erik and he fought to hold his anger in check.

When all had entered, the steward motioned for Erik to follow him inside, then led him to a bench against the southern wall. Directly across the hall from him sat the empty High Seat. "All rise for the king," called the steward.

Every person in the room stood and peered down the hall as two servants escorted Harald into the room from a doorway off to Erik's left. Two low fires burned in the hearths in the center of the room, partially blocking Erik's view of his father as he entered. Yet even through the wavering smoke, Erik could see the effort and strain on the old man's face, and his own heart wrenched at the sight.

"Seat yourselves," instructed the chief steward as Harald finally reached the High Seat. "Erik. Come forward."

As instructed, Erik strode across the hall, aware now of the eyes that scrutinized him. He stopped two paces before the High Seat. As he did so, he marked the low table to the left of the king upon which rested the bejeweled horn of inheritance. Its silver rim twinkled in the light of the two hearth fires, beckoning him to take it in his grasp.

"Kneel," Harald's voice boomed in the quiet interior.

Erik obeyed.

Harald grabbed the golden band on his brow, pulled it clear of his white hair, and slowly lowered it onto Erik's brow. Erik's heart pounded at the feel of the cold metal on his forehead, but his excitement was short-lived, for Harald suddenly lost his balance and placed his hand on Erik's shoulder for balance. Erik reached up to steady his father, heat rising in his cheeks at his sire's weakness.

Harald nodded his thanks and stepped back from his son. "Rise," he commanded, "and take the High Seat."

Erik stepped up to the oaken chair and turned to face the room. Then, with utmost care and a nervous exhalation, he sat on the smooth wooden seat.

The steward placed the horn in Harald's outstretched hands. Carefully, Harald took the vessel and raised it to Erik. "From the womb of giants and gods alike has grown and flourished a race of kings. And like a giant oak, that race has spread its branches and roots of dominance throughout the North, and throughout Midgard. You, my son, are the next in that line of kings. I bid you, do not take it for granted, and remember always that your power lies in the hands of those who granted it to you — the gods." Harald lifted the horn over his head. "With the gods as my witness, I relinquish my High Seat to the care of my son, Erik. I beseech you, my gods, grant him in his kingship the wisdom of Odin, the strength of Thor, the vigilance of Heimdall, and the cunning of Loki." Harald then lowered the vessel to his lips and drank deeply of the liquid within.

Erik took the horn from his father's hands and rose to his feet. "Noble Father, I thank you for the trust you have bestowed upon me. Let it be heard by all that I will rule your kingdom as you yourself ruled, and I will guard with my life all that you worked so hard to create."

Erik turned to the men who lined the hall, instantly marking their expectant gazes. They had a right to be nervous, he thought, for he planned to replace many of those old nobles with his own lords when his father finally died. "Noble lords and family. I ask you to accept me as your king and to follow me as you followed my father. If you do, I can promise that you will want for nothing and that you will live as you have always lived under Harald." It was a lie, but it needed to be said.

He lifted the vessel above his head and gazed into the shadows beyond the roof beams. "Gods above. I thank you for the gift you have bestowed upon me and humbly ask you to grant me all that I might need to rule this kingdom well." He dripped some of the horn's contents onto the hall's floor as a small offering for his request before bringing the vessel to his lips.

"Come forth," the chief steward called after Erik replaced the horn on its stand, "and kneel to your new king."

Chapter 2

Alrekstad Estate, Aarstad, Norway. May, AD 933

Gunnhild awoke in a panic, sweat dripping from her raven-black bangs despite the chill in the room. Her frenzied thoughts struggled for a few wretched moments to dispel the sleep that clung like pitch to her mind. Slowly, her eyes adjusted to the hearth-lit room and focused on the heaving mass of Erik's chest. She frowned jealously. The man could sleep through Ragnarok.

She sat up slowly and ran her long fingers through her tangled hair, allowing her eyes to adjust to the shapes that filled the sleeping chamber. Beside her, on a small table, sat a glass goblet of water. She drank thirstily.

"Did the Night Mare visit you again?" Her husband's voice came as a groggy whisper. He had not moved, and spoke with his eyes shut.

"Aye, husband. That makes thrice that she has come to steal my sleep since the new moon. Something is amiss."

"It was the same dream, then?"

"Aye. It was."

Erik rolled over. "Will you tell me this time what you dreamed?"

Gunnhild studied his face in the half-light of the room. At moments like this, it was hard to believe that this man was the same ruthless warrior who had stolen her from her home so long ago or the man to which Harald Fairhair had entrusted the North three winters before. "Bloodaxe," they called him, though with his mess of fiery red hair and his worried eyes, the byname did not fit. She almost pitied him, for though strong and capable, he had never understood the dreams and magic that were such a large part of her life.

She stroked his cheek with a long, graceful finger and began to describe the visions that had been plaguing her mind. "I dream always of a clearing surrounded by trees. In that clearing stands an oak, tall and wide. When I look for its branches, I cannot see them, for they are lost in the clouds. It is always dusk and the sun is disappearing in the west, across an expanse of water. A mild wind is blowing and things seem peaceful enough. But suddenly, I see flames in the trees that surround the clearing. Off in the direction of the setting sun. And suddenly I can hear the baying of hounds in the distance.

"It seems like a few hounds," she continued, "but I fear that there are more. And the more I fret, the more hounds I hear. It is as if my fear is spawning more and more of those frightful creatures."

Her voice had quickened unintentionally and Erik laid a clammy paw on her arm to settle her. She exhaled deeply and continued.

"The baying is closer now and as it approaches, so too do the flames in the trees. The fire is following the dogs. Through the trees I see them coming toward the clearing, yellow fangs dripping with poison, their eyes the color of blue ice. Dogs from the frozen wastes of Hel's kingdom."

Erik's eyes had opened wide beneath his heavy red brows, his large forehead lined with concern. "A large oak, you say?"

"Aye. Does that mean something to you, husband?"

He pursed his lips. "I have heard our family line being called thus, though I am sure there is no relevance to your dream. A coincidence," he mumbled, though his eyes told a different tale. "Is that all, Gunnhild?"

"There is more, but you are troubled. I think it better that I hold my tongue."

He snorted softly. "Your dream paints a hideous picture, but it does not compare to the things I have seen."

His was the realm of battle, she knew. Frightful and blood-soaked. Hers, the realm of sorcery and the subconscious. Inexplicable and dark. She knew he would never understand her world, but she smiled patiently at his brave words nonetheless. Then she continued. "At the head of the formation of hounds is a golden boar, his tusks longer than any I have ever seen. Together they charge into the clearing, headed straight for me and the great oak. I try to run but my feet are rooted to the soil. The animals come closer, leaving a trail of burned earth where they tread.

"When they reach me, they stop and surround both the tree and me. Then the golden boar lowers his head and rams the oak. The mighty tree shudders but remains rooted. Again the boar rams it, then again. All I can do is witness the grievous display. There are tears on my cheek, though I do not know if they are tears of sorrow or tears of fright. Eventually the great oak succumbs to its foe and crashes to the earth beside me. When it falls, it groans and the earth begins to bleed where the roots have rent the earth. The animals are suddenly gone, but I am up to my ankles in blood. I begin to scream and that is when I awaken."

Erik sat for a long moment, as if attempting to find reason in the images that roamed in his mind. "You have given thought to this dream of yours?"

"Aye husband, but for all my powers, it is beyond my understanding. The Finns taught me well, but I was only their pupil for three winters before you came and stole me away. My powers do not reach that far into the world of the unknown. I can only speculate and that does us no great good."

Erik grunted in agreement. "On the morrow you shall visit Arnkell the Wise and see if you can discover its meaning." He rubbed the soft ivory skin of her arm with a calloused hand. "In the meantime, try to rest."

Gunnhild slid back down under the thick skins that lay upon the bed, knowing well that rest had long slipped from her grasp.

Chapter 3

After the morning meal, a group of Erik's hirdmen escorted Gunnhild northeast into the woods that lay behind Erik's estate. Few ventured alone into those trees, for they encircled the mountain called Ulriken, which cast a sinister and ever-present shadow upon the canopy of pines. More than that, the shadowy forest was home to wild beasts and strange hermits like Arnkell the Wise, the priest who administered the ceremonies on Erik's estate. It was the perfect place for the quiet, misunderstood godi to live, a place where he could spend his days practicing his dark art beyond the prying eyes of any that might be brave enough, or fool enough, to venture near his home.

As the group marched into the woods, Gunnhild's mind turned to the previous night and the dream that plagued her. The dream had kept her awake until the morning, tormenting her with images that persisted even now. And yet, what bothered her was not so much the actual images, but the meaning behind those images and the inexplicable feeling that she was heading toward something beyond her control.

Slowly the path angled up and away from Erik's estate, and Gunnhild thanked the gods that the rain that had so recently visited the land had decided to hold off this day. Eventually her mind turned to the sounds and sights of the forest: the songs of larks and robins, the rays of light that shot down through the canopy of summer leaves like magical, dancing pillars. She had always loved the forest. Something about its power and unseen dangers stimulated her senses and made her feel alive. She supposed it was the same attraction that drew her to Erik.

By midmorning, the group arrived at Arnkell's dwelling, no more than a dilapidated shed that stood on a small rise. Chunks of daub had fallen away from its walls, exposing the vertical pine beams and interwoven wicker. A tiny wisp of smoke drifted from a hole in the tattered thatch that was its roof, carrying with it the smell of boiled onions. Behind the shack and half-hidden among the trees was another such dwelling that Arnkell used as a storage shed for his food and his herbs. In the space between the two structures, Arnkell had built a small pen that housed a couple of chickens and a few goats. These last announced Gunnhild's arrival with a shake of their heads that rang the bells fastened to their necks.

"Wait here," she instructed Erik's warriors. "I will not be long."

The bent figure of Arnkell appeared at the doorway of his home before Gunnhild was halfway across the small clearing. He squinted in her direction as he scratched the long wisps of gray hair that clung to his pointed chin. In one hand he held a gnarled staff upon which he leaned, while from the other hung a long-handled knife with a curved blade. "Who is there?"

Gunnhild stopped and smiled. "Have no fear, Arnkell. It is I, Gunnhild. I have brought some supplies." She removed the sack from her back and held it out to him, though she knew Arnkell could not see it from this distance.

Arnkell's toothless mouth twisted upward into a grin as he stepped forward to greet her. "I expected you earlier, my lady." His voice cracked with age.

Long ago she had learned not to be alarmed by Arnkell's powers of foresight. It was a harmless gift that could not be explained, or taught, and only came in handy for occurrences as mundane as expecting visitors or forecasting weather.

She kissed his prickly, weatherworn cheek. "Your skills must be getting rusty, then."

"Hah! Rusty, you say. My eyesight might leave me. My hearing might go. But death will take me before my skills falter." He turned and walked with Gunnhild toward his home. "So tell me. What brings my favorite student out today?"

"A dream."

"A premonition?"

Gunnhild shrugged as she ducked under the doorway and stepped into the musty darkness beyond. "Perchance a premonition. Perchance not. That is what I have come to find out."

Arnkell grunted his understanding, then moved to the cauldron that hung from a tripod over his small hearth. He grabbed the long spoon within it and stirred a few times. While he did, Gunnhild looked around at the dwelling she knew so well. Beyond the hearth, on the opposite side of the room from the doorway, lay a small bed of straw covered with a bearskin blanket. Two three-legged stools, one short, the other tall, rested on either side of the fire. Next to the tall stool, and illuminated in the eerie glow of two cod-oil lamps, stood a long table upon which were spread clumps of herbs, roots, and dried flowers, vessels of all shapes and sizes, and a small hand-quern. More dried herbs and flowers hung from two ropes that stretched down opposite walls.

Gunnhild moved to the table and cleared a space for the supplies she'd brought: a thick wool blanket and a new cloak. "I thought you might be able to use these."

Arnkell moved to the table and peered at the gifts, then ran the material of the blanket between his gnarled thumb and forefinger. "Soft."

She smiled, knowing that the small compliment was the only thanks she would receive. "One of my women made them. She has a special way with wool."

Arnkell grunted and moved back to the fire. "Are you hungry? I have made some goat's blood broth with onion and radishes."

Gunnhild politely declined.

Arnkell grabbed a bowl that lay beside the fire and held it over the cauldron. Slowly, he spooned the broth into the bowl, then sat on the small stool and began to slurp at his meal. After two such slurps, he looked at Gunnhild and pointed to the larger stool with his spoon. "Bring the stool over here, Gunnhild, and tell me of this dream."

Gunnhild did what she was told and recounted the dream to Arnkell exactly as she remembered it, leaving no detail unspoken. Arnkell listened in silence, interrupting only to spoon more of the broth into his toothless mouth.

When she was through, Arnkell nodded in understanding. "And you would like to know if this dream portends something ominous?"

Gunnhild nodded.

Arnkell scratched at his thinning beard and worked his jaw in a rotating manner like a chewing cow. Then, without a word, he stood and moved to the table, where he shifted through the mess until he located what he was looking for: a small leather pouch. He fumbled with the pouch's strings until he had it open, whereupon he emptied the contents into a small clay vessel.

This he carried back to the fire and handed to Gunnhild.

As she expected, it contained a number of ivory squares, yellowed with age, upon which were carved different runic inscriptions. These were Arnkell's runes and the most prized possession in his home. They were an heirloom from his father, who in turn had received them from his own father, and on down the line as far back as the dawn of time. The ability to read the stones was a gift possessed only by a small number of people, and received, so men said, directly from Odin, the first being ever to use runes. Gunnhild had learned the craft while living with the godi in Finnmark, but was by no means a master.

While she fingered the runes delicately, Arnkell held his curved blade over the flames until the metal glowed orange from the heat. "Give me your finger," he commanded gently.

Gunnhild did as she was told, though she tensed in anticipation of the pain she knew would soon follow. Deftly, Arnkell brought the blade to Gunnhild's finger and drew it quickly across her skin. She sucked in her breath involuntarily as a drop of blood bubbled up where the blade had been. Holding the bowl between her legs, she grabbed her finger and pressed until nine drops had fallen onto the runes. Nine was the magical number of Odin, for He had hung nine days from the World Tree, Yggdrasil, where the runes first came to his possession.

Gunnhild handed the bowl to Arnkell, who stuck his fingers into it and mixed the blood with the runes. As he did so, his ancient voice mumbled the incantation spoken by Odin so long ago:

> *"Runes you will find and rightly read,*
> *of wondrous weight,*
> *of mighty magic,*
> *which I have dyed with my blood,*
> *which were made by the holy host,*
> *and were etched by me."*

Nine times Arnkell repeated the incantation. When he finished, he beckoned to Gunnhild. She moved to his side and knelt. "Close your eyes and concentrate on the images of your dream. When you are ready, choose three runes from the bowl."

She did so and placed them in a horizontal line before her, inscribed side down.

Arnkell bent over the runes and flipped the first, which represented Gunnhild's present situation. The old godi fingered it carefully, his jaw once again in motion. "*Inguz*. I see this in your dream."

"How?"

"The tree that falls can be looked at as ancient, or as 'the old way.' *Inguz* is a sign of change or a signal that the old ways are about to end. Your dream and this rune are closely related."

"I must be prepared, then, for change?"

Arnkell held up a finger to stop her. "It is more complicated than that."

Gunnhild looked at him, confused.

"Think of change as a layer of ice upon a lake. Change is the ice. Dangerous, yes, but manageable, if you are prepared. That which lies beneath is the real threat to your safety, for it is that water below that can kill you. Spoken another way, you must be prepared for change, but more importantly, you must be prepared for that which spawns that change. You see, change is unalterable — its course has already been woven by the Norns. Do you understand?"

Gunnhild nodded. "Aye."

"Good. Now, flip the next rune."

The second rune stood for the action to be taken as a result of the first rune. Gunnhild did as she was told, aware now of the beating in her chest. She recognized it instantly and understood without having to be told that the message here was danger.

Arnkell confirmed her thoughts. "*Hagalaz.* The rune of disruption."

"The change will bring disruption." Gunnhild struggled to contain her anxiety, but her trembling voice betrayed her.

Arnkell scratched his chin, then rose and moved to a jug that stood on the table. He grabbed two cups, blew into them to remove the dust, then poured some of the jug's contents into each. Without a word he shuffled back to the stool and sat, then passed Gunnhild a cup. Before speaking, he drank deeply of his own. When he was through, he pointed his chin at Gunnhild. "Drink. It will calm you."

Gunnhild's impatience bubbled. "I have no wish for calm. What does this rune mean?"

He sighed heavily. "In the context of your dream, it means that the falling of the great oak will disrupt. Be that gradually or quickly, I do not know. But the rune you have drawn can be as subtle as a realization or as powerful as a complete life change. In other words, death in one form or another. Flip the last rune."

"Death?"

"Careful," Arnkell warned. "I said death in one form or another. Not all death is bad. Does the caterpillar not die when it becomes a butterfly? Do new shoots not grow from frozen ground?"

Gunnhild was not calmed by Arnkell's comparisons and frowned deeply.

"Come now," Arnkell urged. "Flip the third one."

Her heart sat in her throat as she unveiled the third rune.

"*Ehwaz.* Movement."

Gunnhild studied Arnkell's face. "I do not understand."

"Nor do I. All I can glean is that this disruption will force this movement, which, as you know, can be physical or mental in nature. A new way of thinking. Or a new dwelling place."

"But how does all this together tie to my dream?"

Arnkell took another long draught from his cup, then spat at the fire. It hissed back at him. For a long time, he stared into the flames, until Gunnhild began to wonder if he'd ever answer her question. She opened her mouth to interrupt his thoughts, but Arnkell held up a hand and stilled her. "Silence. I am thinking."

Angered by the rebuke, Gunnhild tipped her own cup to her lips and made to drink, but withdrew her face sharply when she smelled what swirled inside. She glanced into the cup but could not discern its contents. Whatever it was, it smelled strong and sour. Disgusted, yet mindful of her host's feelings, she set the cup aside.

"I believe your dream to be the portent of a monumental change, a change wrought by the fall of the giant oak. In my mind, that oak represents a king, and the boar, his claimant to the throne. The boar will have a large army and will spill the blood of all who stand in his way. This change will disrupt your life, though for better or worse is not clear. And in the end it will require a move, though what sort of move I do not know."

"My husband's lineage has been called a great oak. My husband told me so," she whispered when she had regained her wits. She gazed at Arnkell. "Is he to fail? Is another line of kings to rise?"

Arnkell raised his old hands. "Careful. We know not what fate the Norns have woven for your husband. Not even the gods know. What we do know is that your husband is, in name and title, king of the North after Harald's abdication. But his brothers have also named themselves kings in their respective lands. Now, Harald yet lives, and as long as he lives, his sons, including your husband, are content to accumulate their power where they rule. When Harald dies, your husband and his brothers will vie for the High Seat, for that is the way of things. So then, at this point there is only one true king to fall. Harald. I believe him to be the tree at the center of the forest, for it was he who spread his seed far and wide and it is his rule under which we all live, like plants beneath an oak. Do you understand my words?"

Gunnhild smiled, feeling somewhat eased by the old man's explanation. "So you think that the fallen king will be Harald?"

"Aye." Arnkell sat quietly for a moment. "I am rather certain of it."

"How can you be certain?"

Arnkell focused on Gunnhild. "Have you ever heard the tale of Queen Ragnhild's tree?"

Gunnhild knew only that Queen Ragnhild was Harald Fairhair's mother and that Gunnhild's own daughter had been named for the woman. "I know only a few details of her, but I know nothing of a tale about a tree."

"Ah," Arnkell said. "Then let me tell you. Like you, Ragnhild dreamed, and it was said that quite often these dreams came to pass. In one dream, Ragnhild was standing in her garden and plucked a thorn from her gown. As she held it, the thorn grew, so much so that one end went into the ground and became deeply rooted. The other end grew higher than the eye could see. So high that it vanished into the clouds. It was said that the nethermost part of the tree was blood red and that its branches spread all over the North and farther still. Does this tree sound familiar to you?"

Gunnhild nodded dumbly.

"Shortly after this dream, Queen Ragnhild and King Halvdan had a boy child, whom they named Harald." Arnkell finished the story with a lift of his eyebrows and a long draught from his cup.

"That is a strange coincidence," murmured Gunnhild.

Arnkell grinned. "I believe it is more than a coincidence."

Gunnhild nodded. "If Harald is the oak, who then will be his successor? The boar?"

At this, Arnkell smiled his toothless smile. "Think you for a moment. Did you not say the boar comes from the direction of the setting sun? The west?"

"Aye."

"Which of Harald's three sons now ruling in the North resides in the west? Which son has been chosen to rule upon Harald's death?"

Gunnhild's heart leapt. "Erik!"

Arnkell nodded. "Aye. Now, bring me some more of that mead. My throat hurts from all this talking."

Gunnhild guffawed as she stood. "Mead, you call that?"

"Hah! Then if you think it bad, bring some the next time you require my services. I am tiring of your cloaks and blankets."

Chapter 4

Gunnhild sat at her loom and worked her long fingers about the threads, her dark brows bent in concentration. At her side stood her daughter Ragnhild, who adeptly dislodged thread from the distaff she held between her long neck and skinny shoulders. At Gunnhild's feet sat her young son Harald, who had recently celebrated his second Yule and now stuffed bits of bread into his mouth so that his cheeks bulged like a squirrel's. Across from them, Erik sat on his chair among several of his hirdmen, running a whetstone down the blade of his battle-axe. The grating noise made it hard for Gunnhild to focus.

"When do we sup, Gunnhild?" called Erik from his chair.

Gunnhild cursed under her breath at the interruption. "It would come sooner if I were allowed to concentrate on my weaving. How is the thread coming, child?"

Her daughter, Ragnhild, shrugged. "Well enough. I am almost ready to wind it."

Gunnhild nodded approvingly. Ragnhild was a quick study and showed a lot of promise in the skills of the house. She would make a fine wife to someone when she reached the marrying age.

Erik interrupted again. "Gunnhild. How went your visit with Arnkell?"

She cursed again and sighed. Forgetting her loom, she turned to her husband, trying to gauge his disposition. Content that his inquiry was sincere, she answered, "Well."

Erik leaned his great axe against the side of his chair and motioned his hirdmen away.

"Leave us in peace," Gunnhild said to her children. "Your father and I must speak in private."

Ragnhild looked from her mother to her father, set down her distaff and spindle, then guided young Harald from the hall. Erik's hirdmen and thralls obediently followed. When they had gone, Erik leaned forward in his seat.

"It was good to hear his words," she began, "though hard, as well." She knew the closeness Erik shared with his father, and therefore that her tale required delicacy in its telling.

Concern shrouded Erik's features. "Why hard?"

"Arnkell said that the tree in the clearing is a king and that the boar is that king's successor."

Erik's eyes remained fixed on his wife, but he did not speak.

Gunnhild forged ahead. "Arnkell believes that the king, husband, is your father, and you are the boar, or successor." Gunnhild clenched her jaw in expectation of Erik's reaction.

Erik's brows bent over his eyes. "Did not the boar topple the oak? Am I to overthrow my father?"

"No. Arnkell did not see that. He cited several reasons why he believes your father to be the oak, including a story about your mother that seemed to match my dream."

Erik blanched. "I had forgotten that tale."

Gunnhild nodded. "He said also that the boar comes from the west."

Erik's concern transformed to confusion. "I do not understand. What has the west to do with it?"

"Everything," she explained patiently. "The boar came from the direction of the setting sun. The west. Of all of Harald's remaining sons, you alone reside and rule in the west of the land. For that reason, Arnkell believes the boar to be you."

Erik's face softened. "And what say you? Do you believe his words?"

"I have no reason to doubt what he says."

Erik sighed. "It is as I suspected, though it is never welcome news to hear. Harald's passing will be a tough draught to swallow and I do not relish the day when it comes. Yet I cannot deny the bittersweet thought, for it portends my succession."

"Aye, Erik. It does."

Just then, young Gamle burst into the hall, his head bandaged from a fall he had recently taken. He was seven winters old, chestnut-haired and dull-eyed like a troll, with a bulbous nose that sat like a boulder in the middle of his round face. He ran across the hall, tripped on a table leg, recovered, then bowed deeply before his father.

"What is it, Gamle? Can you not see your mother and I speak to each other in private?" Erik's voice bristled.

"Father, I…I have brought most grievous news."

Erik glanced at Gunnhild, then turned back to his son with a scowl. "Well? Out with it."

"Your father…" he blurted, then swallowed and tried again. "Your father has joined the Einherjar of Valhall. He died six days ago."

Erik paused, his gray eyes searching those of his son, his fists ever so slowly unclenching. Gunnhild sat motionless.

Erik turned his eyes to his wife's face, his brows raised in disbelief, then turned back to his son. "And how came you by this news, Gamle?"

"By me, my lord."

Erik's foster brother, Arinbjorn, bent his large frame through the doorway. Behind him trailed Ragnvald, Erik's oldest son. Now in his fifteenth summer, he stood nearly as tall as Arinbjorn's shoulder. He spoke when the two entered. "Arinbjorn retrieved me from Herle to help bring the news to you. He figured you would want me here. Gamle met us on the beach and we sent him ahead to bring the news to you." His adolescent voice cracked.

Arinbjorn crossed the hall in four long strides and knelt before the High Seat. "I am sorry for your loss, my friend. I know you were his favorite. But he has moved on to Valhall, a better place for a warrior such as him."

Erik's angular face had turned ashen.

"My lord?" Arinbjorn asked.

"Gunnhild has seen this death in her dreams and was just explaining it to me when you brought the news."

Arinbjorn looked at Gunnhild, making no attempt to conceal his own superstitious wonder. He quickly composed himself and bowed in greeting.

She inclined her head to acknowledge him, then turned back to her husband. "I am sorry for your loss, husband," she offered, straightening the wrinkles in her overdress unconsciously as she spoke. "Arinbjorn and his men will be hungry," she added. "I will leave you two in peace and start preparing a meal."

Within the hour, Alrekstad was filled with well wishers, though despite the crowd, it remained uncomfortably still. Erik's hirdmen sat quietly about the hearth, concentrating on their own tasks and hushed conversations. Across from them, Arinbjorn's men ate in silence, vigilantly watching their leader between slurps of stew and gulps of ale. Ragnvald sat at his father's knee, while his sister Ragnhild quietly directed the thralls to replenish drinking horns and trenchers. The only form of entertainment was Erik's young sons, Guthorm and Gamle, who danced about the group, swinging their wooden swords at each other in make-believe battle. Harald, still too young to understand the significance of the visitors but sensing the tension, fidgeted on his mother's lap and slapped a wooden spoon against the table.

"What word of my brothers, Arinbjorn? Do they know of my father's death?"

Arinbjorn pulled his face from the drinking horn and sleeved the ale from his white-blond mustache. "If they do not, they will know soon enough. On his deathbed, King Harald willed each of his hirdmen to spread the news. The whole land will know in a matter of days."

Erik stroked his fiery beard. "And how came you by the information so quickly?"

"I was there, attending to another matter. On his last breath, I hastened to you to bring the news."

Erik considered this as he toyed with the meat within his trencher. "It seems my father wishes to test my strength even before his body is cold. As surely as Thor creates the thunder, there will be unrest with my brothers."

"Does that worry you, husband? Ragnhild! Mind the boys!"

Guthorm and Gamle had let their battle come perilously close to the hearth. Ragnhild raced to cut them off before Gamle stepped on a burning log or knocked the cauldron from its stand.

"Worry me? It does not worry me to trade sword strokes with any man, kinsman or no. As everyone knows, I have already been the banesman to two of my brothers." Erik turned back to his guest. "Arinbjorn. What think you? Will my half-brothers move against me?"

Arinbjorn deliberated for a few silent moments. "I know not whether they will attack straightaway or if they will come together. But of the three remaining in the land, two are dangerous men. Olav was brother to Bjorn the Chapman, whom you killed on your father's orders. He may be content in the Vestfold, but he may also fear that you will move preemptively to take his realm, given the richness of that fylke in both trade and agriculture. Halvdan, of course, is the other. He is a fighter. Under Harald, he was protected and enjoyed the uninhibited rule of the Trondelag. He will not trust you to offer him the same, and rightfully so." He glanced into Erik's face to see if he had offended his host, but Erik's face remained benign. "My worry is not so much Halvdan by himself, but Halvdan with help from the others. He is not strong enough to come against you, but if he can rally supporters to his side, than we will have problems."

"Olav?"

Arinbjorn shrugged his massive shoulders. "Olav or Jarl Ivar in the Uplands. Or both."

"What of Sigfrid? He also sits up in the Trondelag with Halvdan."

Arinbjorn snorted derisively. "Sigfrid is a weakling. A man more content to eat and drink and screw than fight. It is Halvdan that we should fear."

"Then we must rid ourselves of Halvdan."

Gunnhild's words brought a stillness to the already silent hall. Erik poked a chunk of meat and examined it, nodding as he did so. "Aye. You are right, Gunnhild. Yet I am reluctant to call out an army so soon before my father's funeral."

Gunnhild grinned. "There are more ways to kill a man that meeting him in battle."

The suggestion made men look away, though none gainsaid Gunnhild. She looked at their uncomfortable faces and almost laughed. Warriors were so simple-minded. They knew how to stab with their swords and smash their shields, but the mere mention of anything more complicated, and less honorable, made their skin crawl. She glanced at her husband and noted that he among them was not hiding his eyes. Rather, he nodded at her.

So be it, then. She would deal with Halvdan.

Chapter 5

Haugesund, Norway. May, AD 933

The clouds hung low and dark over Harald's favorite estate at Haugesund, a fitting sky for the burial of one of the North's most renowned kings. A chilling wind swept up the gentle rise from the sea to the clearing where the crowd had gathered, carrying with it the scent of salt and a gentle drizzle that had begun to fall. Tiny droplets of water hung from the leafy branches of the trees surrounding the clearing, dripping slowly onto the heads of those gathered to see Harald Fairhair laid to rest.

"Odin mourns," murmured someone from the crowd.

"Nay," corrected another. "He is shedding tears of joy. For now King Harald has joined Him in Valhall, and there he shall regale the dead with his tales."

Before them, in a massive pit, lay a longship, its dragon-headed prow removed and placed inside the ship for fear it would frighten the gods on arrival in the afterlife. A wooden shelter had been constructed in the middle of the ship to house the body of the mightiest king the North had ever known. Strewn about the ship were beautifully painted shields and spears, finely made swords and axes, cooking utensils, barrels of mead and wine, and victuals of all sorts. At the foot of King Harald's shelter lay the body of one of his concubines, who had volunteered to die with her master and accompany him into the world beyond. Beside her lay King Harald's beautiful white steed, as well as the three Irish hounds given to him by the king of the Dubhlinn Norse. Harald would arrive in the hall of the heroes as he had lived his life: as a king.

When the sons of Harald had each said some words at the edge of the grave, the gravediggers began to fill in the burial pit with the rain-soaked earth. The rain began to fall in earnest now, and the less hearty onlookers retired to the hall at Haugesund to find some warmth.

Sigurd, the jarl of Lade, watched solemnly as the cloaked figures slowly retreated, his long auburn mane and beard soaked and matted to his head and chest. Drops of salty rain dripped down his forehead and into his ice-blue eyes. He swiped sourly at a drop that hung from the tip of his broken nose. Across the pit from him, the sons of Harald stood motionless, heads down-turned, their dark cloaks waving heavily in the breeze as Harald's ship disappeared beneath the gravediggers' mud. Sigurd knew their shapes. The barrel-chested, broad-shouldered form of Erik. The short, round body of his own king, Sigfrid. And the giant, Olav. Unlike himself, products of different women but the same man, the king now being covered with earth. Sigurd edged closer to them.

Jarl Sigurd was the son of Harald Fairhair's good friend and a kinsman to Harald through marriage. Sigfrid may have been king of the Trondelag, but it was the jarl's family that wielded the true power in that far northern realm. It was they who controlled trade with the Finns and commanded the support of the people — known as the Tronds — in their district. Before Sigfrid, it had been Halvdan who ruled as king. But at a recent feast, his heart had suddenly stopped beating in his chest, killing him right there at the table beside his wife. A quick investigation of his plate and cup proved that he had been poisoned. Fearing inner strife among their own nobles, Jarl Sigurd and his supporters had acted quickly and elected the rotund and physically inept Sigfrid in Halvdan's stead. Though not the model king of their land, he possessed more right than any other to serve as king of the Tronds.

"Jarl Sigurd! Why do you stand there like a grave robber? Come join us." Erik's voice shattered Sigurd's thoughts and brought him back to the present.

Sigurd flinched at the insult but held his anger in check. He walked over to the group and placed his hand on Olav's shoulder in greeting, but passed purposefully over Erik.

Erik smiled wickedly at the gesture. "Have you learned no manners in Lade?"

Sigurd's eyes narrowed. "Aye. But greeting whoresons is not one of them."

Erik grinned evilly. "I see you are angry at me. For the death of Halvdan, perchance? I suppose it does not matter to you that it was not my doing."

"Aye. I suppose you, a man who has already killed several of his brothers, would never kill another kinsman." Sigurd's voice oozed sarcasm.

Erik straightened. "Those deaths were necessary and ordered by my father."

Sigurd shrugged his round shoulders. "You have killed two brothers already. What is a third to you?"

Erik made for his sword, but Olav grabbed his arm before he could reach it. "As much as I love a good fight, this is not the day for fighting."

It was Sigfrid who spoke next, trying his best to ease the tension. Beneath the hood of his cloak, his cheeks looked like two red apples. "Any word from Dag or Ring?"

"I fear," answered Olav, "that our brothers met their death in the East. I know that Dag fell near Holmgard. There was a rumor that Ring was alive and fighting in the army of the Rus, but no one has been able to confirm that."

"That is a shame," mumbled Sigfrid with a deep sigh.

A silence fell on the men. It was not the comfortable silence of good friends, but the pained quiet of hostile men when all cordiality has been exhausted. Beside them, the gravediggers had only half completed their task and much of the ship was still visible in the muddy pit. On the morrow, the thralls would complete the task by building a large mound to mark the spot.

Erik broke the silence. "Come. Let us find some warmth. There is much I wish to discuss."

Erik led the three men to a smaller hall that stood beside the main one. It was old and dilapidated and smelled of must. Rain dripped from holes in the thatch, forming large pools on the floor. A small fire crackled at one end of the hall, casting its heat on the table and benches that sat in the middle of the dwelling. Several large pitchers and cups stood in the middle of a long table. Erik motioned the men to take their seats, then began filling each man's cup. As he did, Arinbjorn stepped from the shadows near the door. Sigurd saw him first and rose quickly to his feet.

Erik motioned him down. "Please, Jarl Sigurd, sit. I have asked Arinbjorn to join us. I hope that is agreeable."

Reluctantly, Sigurd reclaimed his seat but pushed away his cup. He noted the others left their cups untouched as well. Only Erik lifted his, and after taking a long guzzle, addressed them.

"It gladdens me that you are all here. I did not think you would come."

This brought a snort from Olav, whose height gave him the appearance, even as he sat, of standing. "Do you think that we do not mourn the passing of our father?"

"That is not what he meant, Olav." Sigfrid had shed his cloak, revealing the true size of his girth, which spread itself in great rolls across the bench and threatened to tear the seams of his rich garments. "We meant only to pay homage to our lost father, Erik. But we were not so half-witted to think that you would not try something. We have no plans to stay the night."

Erik considered this briefly as he sipped his ale. "In this weather?"

Olav spoke now. "We have all seen worse. Now then, let us stop this babble. What is the purpose of this meeting, Erik? If it is to make peace with us, or inform us of your overlordship, then you are wasting you breath and our time. You have proved, even before your ascension to the High Seat, that your motives are self-serving and that you care little for the true health of this realm. I think the murder of my brother Bjorn, who brought more wealth to this land than any of us, proved that point well. But Halvdan's untimely death has driven the nail home.

"While Father was alive, we paid our taxes and abided by his rule. In exchange, he stayed out of our way and let us rule our fylke, so long as that rule did not come into conflict with his own. But when you ascended to the High Seat, things changed. Your ships prey on our traders. You drive Father's nobles away and replace them with your own. You make a mockery of our law assemblies with those very same nobles. While Father lived, we were powerless to stop you, knowing full well you enjoyed his backing and support." As he spoke, his voice gained in pitch and his cheeks reddened.

"But now Father is gone and you are on your own. Father's men, loyal to him as they were bound by oath to be, have no loyalties to you. Some have begun to reject you. I know because some have come to me. Others to Sigfrid." Olav smiled victoriously. "That levels the field and makes it easier for us to say what we must to you

— that we will no longer recognize your rule or submit to your will. Our borders will be closed to both your tax collectors and your pirates. Henceforth, consider the Vestfold and Trondelag no longer part of your kingdom."

Erik's face waxed redder with each word that came from his brother's mouth. Finally he could take no more and slammed his fist onto the table, toppling one of the pitchers and spilling its ale across the boards and onto the muddy floor. When he spoke, his voice sounded choked. "Those fylke are mine to rule, given to me lawfully by our father. Just as his High Seat was given to me. If you defy me, and defy the law, you will leave me with no choice but to crush you both like worms beneath my boot."

Olav shrugged. "We will take our chances."

Erik scowled. "So be it, then. Come, Arinbjorn. We know now where we stand with my brothers." Erik stormed from the hall with Arinbjorn on his heel.

Olav turned to the table when he was gone and smiled through his brown beard. "Well. That went well."

Sigfrid frowned and let his beefy shoulders sag. "Alas. The time has come. I had hoped we would never see such a day."

Beside him, Jarl Sigurd twirled his cup in his hands. "We will need to make our plans quickly. Erik will not tarry for long."

Olav stood. "Then let us be away from this wretched place and start our planning."

Chapter 6

Tunsberg, Vestfold. Late July, AD 933

"Erik is coming, I tell you. We are not yet fully prepared." Sigfrid made no attempt to hide his consternation.

Jarl Sigurd frowned. Having been raised with Sigfrid, he was used to the man's fretting. Still, he did not like it, even if his king did have the right of it.

Olav could not have been more different in nature; he scoffed at his half-brother. "We have Mollebakken, Sigfrid," he protested, motioning vaguely in the direction of the hill that rose to the east of his estate. "Let Erik come. He will find us atop that hill and will wish he had not wasted his time. And if he decides to attack us as we stand upon that hill, we will cut him down like the swine that he is."

Though Olav's words silenced Sigfrid, Jarl Sigurd was not so easily impressed. He was seated behind his rotund king and now he stood and drew his bearlike frame to its full height. "It is true that we have your hill on which to fight, and we have scouts watching the approaches to your estate. But the situation is graver than you might think, Olav. As we have told you already, Erik has found support from the Orkneyjar as well as from King Gorm of the Danes. If the numbers being reported about Erik's army are true, we will need more than the hill of Mollebakken and our hird, however stout, to defend ourselves. We will need defensive works and assistance from the locals."

Olav laughed. "That does not speak well of your army then, Jarl Sigurd. My men are the finest fighters in the North," he boasted. "Based on Sigfrid's whining, we have agreed to meet Erik on Mollebakken, though I think my men alone could meet his men on a flat plain and still win the day, eh men?" A chorus of skals met his boast.

Sigurd had to bite his tongue to keep from insulting Olav's blind pride. A man had the right to be proud, but when that pride jeopardized the lives of everyone about him, it became nothing more than folly. "With all respect, Olav, we did not sail from the Trondelag to take chances. We came to crush Erik once and for all time."

Despite the deference of his words, Jarl Sigurd's tone was condescending. Others in the room heard it too and a few looked up in surprise. Sigurd ignored them.

"I advise you watch yourself, jarl," Olav warned. "It may be that you can speak to my mighty brother so," he motioned at the blushing Sigfrid, "but you are in *my* hall and I am *your* host."

"Thank you for the clarification," Sigurd mumbled.

"I only clarify to men who are too daft to grasp it themselves."

Sigfrid held up his hands beseechingly. "Olav. Please. Listen to reason. I know you thirst to cut Erik down, as do we. But if the reports are true, he outnumbers us. We need more defenses and to rally the locals, as Jarl Sigurd says." His jowls shook as he spoke.

Sigurd could almost see his lord's words glance off Olav's high forehead, like blunt arrows off a shield.

"What of the Uplanders?" It was Olav's nephew, Gudrod Bjornsson, who asked the question. His father had been Bjorn the Chapman, whom Erik had killed. Now he lived under Olav's roof as a fosterling. "Can we expect assistance from King Ivar?"

Jarl Sigurd glanced at the boy. "No."

"Why?"

"King Ivar has been busy fighting the Swedes on his borders and can spare no men, or so he says. More likely, he is waiting like a wolf to come take what he can after the fight is over. Whoever wins and loses this fight is no concern to him, so long as he can profit."

Outside, the wind howled as it blew in from the bay, calling to mind the spirits of warriors and the gods of war. Within the hall, the hearth fire snapped and popped, fueled by a gust that had worked its way through the walls and now swirled about the room.

Sigfrid tried one last time. "Brother, please. Listen to reason. We need to prepare our defenses. It is the prudent course."

Olav considered his brother. After a long silence, he stood, straightened his tunic, and studied the men gathered about the hall. "Very well. On the morrow, we shall start to build some defenses and send word to the locals. Now, this discussion has given me a headache and I must retire. I will see you all at daybreak." He downed the dregs in his cup and marched from the room.

Sigurd watched the man go, thanking the gods that he had finally acquiesced. Though a part of him wondered if it was already too late, for Erik was on the move, and from the latest reports, he was close.

In a large bay east of Olav's estate at Tunsberg lay the army of Erik Bloodaxe.

In less than two moons, Erik had assembled an army larger than any he had ever commanded and moved it to within an easy hike of his foe. Nearly thirty ships. Over fifteen hundred men. Most were from his native Rogaland and the neighboring fylker of Hordaland and the Fjord — men anxious to support their king and gain favor in his eyes. Some had come from Denmark, allies only in their thirst for adventure and plunder, and their desire to spill the blood of ancient enemies in Vestfold. Still others had come from as far as the Orkney Islands, or the Orkneyjar. And now all camped here on this nameless shore along the Vik, waiting for the battle and their chance at glory.

The wind had picked up earlier in the evening and now blew fiercely across the fingers of land that protected the bay. In the half-light of the northern summer night, Erik watched it stir the waves into a frenzy of whitecaps and bend the trees that stood like sentries on the islands of the fjord. Every so often a branch would tumble to the ground, torn from its trunk like a limb sliced from a body.

His gaze moved west, toward Tunsberg, and he wondered what his brothers might be doing. Were they alert to his sudden arrival? Would they be waiting for him when he arrived? In a way he hoped they were. He wanted them to be prepared and to die despite that preparation, for they had taken what was rightfully his and deserved to die for their perfidy.

A dark mass of low-lying clouds was gathering to the east. Erik smiled. Thor had come to witness the fight. He had brought with Him his foul weather, but it mattered not — Erik had come too far to turn back now.

Chapter 7

The rain came before the night was through. It began slowly, gentle enough to stir Erik's sleeping army but not rouse them from their slumber. Soon, however, the sky opened up, drowning the last precious minutes of sleep with raindrops the size of stones, awakening the warriors, who responded with bitter curses and grumbles of discontent.

After a cold, fireless morning meal, Erik ordered his warriors to assemble, which they did in shuffling silence. The main force would consist of Erik's warriors — men of Hordaland, Rogaland, and the Fjord — with Erik and his blood-brother Arinbjorn at their head. On the left were the Orkneymen, whose responsibility it was to guard the shoreline either from an unexpected sea assault or from any attempt by the enemy to retreat to their ships. On the inland, or right, flank were the Danes, led by Svein of Jutland, kinsman to the Danish king. The Danes were to swing around to the north as soon as the engagement began and block any attempt to retreat inland.

When the men had organized themselves to Erik's satisfaction, he gave the signal to advance. There were no horn blasts or cheers, no swords beating on shield rims. Erik wanted to approach his half-brother's estate as silently as possible, which, in the downpour, was not silent at all. The men tripped and fumbled their way through the trees in the heavy rain, cursing aloud as they slipped in the ooze or ran headlong into low-lying branches. Visibility was never more than twenty paces in any one direction. Messengers stumbled between the forces to make certain that contact was not lost.

Some of the warriors, certain that this weather was a portent of bad luck, groped at the talismans at their necks. Erik, however, remained optimistic. As long as the torrent kept up, he felt certain that the pounding of the raindrops would mask the sound of his army's advance. In addition, he could be relatively certain that no one would see him coming, for it was highly unlikely that any person with their wits about them would be out in such a downpour. And if they were, they certainly would not be expecting an attack. Still, he took the precaution of avoiding open ground so that even if the rain did stop, his army's movements would be concealed.

By midmorning, they'd reached the edge of the woods on the outskirts of Olav's estate. Erik halted his army to give them time for last-minute preparations. Men besought their favored gods for skill and battle-luck. Others invoked the deities to strengthen their armor and their weapons, or to fetter their foes in the heat of combat. Then, one by one, the grim-faced, rain-drenched men hefted their shields, yanked blades from scabbards, and readied themselves for battle.

"A fine day for the wolf's feast." Sigurd looked up into the rain and pulled his long auburn hair — now wet and smooth — back behind his head. A wide grin brightened his heavy face.

Beside him, Sigfrid shivered. "You act as if the attack comes today, in this torrent. How can you be so certain?"

"I cannot. I only know what I would do, were I Erik." He patted his king on the shoulder with a laugh, then started off for the beach where his men were beginning to assemble.

"So what does that mean? Should we prepare ourselves?" called Sigfrid.

Sigurd stopped and turned. "Aye. It may come to naught, but why risk it? The locals have not yet shown, so let us do what we can before Erik appears. Take your hird and remain on the hilltop with the work group there. Help them prepare the defenses, but be wary of an attack. Keep your shields and weapons to hand. I will help the men here on the beach complete the defenses. Whichever way Erik comes, we want him climbing at us, not encircling us, so these beach defenses need to be strong."

Just that morning, the kings had decided to divide their men into separate work groups to prepare for Erik's attack. Olav's men were sent to chop down trees in the nearby woods to be used as barriers. Half of Sigfrid's men, the Tronds, were tasked with hauling the logs to the top of Mollebakken, which lay just to the west of his estate, while the other half dragged their logs to the beach. Still more men worked to create another barrier on the opposite side of the hill, with the goal of slowing any flanking move by Erik.

Sigurd glanced at the hilltop, wondering for the hundredth time why Olav was so opposed to fighting behind the walls that encircled his estate. He understood that Olav feared being trapped inside or having it burned to the ground when the rains stopped. Those were legitimate concerns. But if Erik's army was really as large as the reports suggested, then fighting in the open — even on a hilltop — was folly. He sighed. "Good luck, Sigfrid."

"And to you, Sigurd."

"What word?" Erik blinked at his messenger through the rain.

"My lord. The enemy does not appear ready. They are spread about and toil at their defensive works. Some work in the woods not far from where the Danes wait. Others drag the wood to the hill near the estate or to the beach below. Not one man is dressed for battle. No helmets. No chain mail. Some do not even carry weapons."

"How many men?"

"Four hundred at most. Mayhap more. I could not count those that work in the woods."

A tinge of guilt shot through Erik's veins as he listened to the words. This, he mused, would be as easy as killing a child. So be it then. Let them die.

Suddenly, a shout rang out in the morning air, ending his reflection. It had come from his right, where the Danes lay in waiting. Erik hefted his battle-axe, pressed past the messenger, and started forward. "Follow me!" he bellowed as his feet carried him through the trees.

The fight for the North had begun.

Chapter 8

In a few quick strides, Erik was out of the woods and sprinting across the field toward Olav's hall. A glance confirmed the truth in all that the messenger had relayed to him. The enemy was there, but not arrayed for battle. Not even dressed for battle. They saw Erik's men and ran helter-skelter for their weapons and shields. To his right, axemen fled before the onslaught of Erik's Danes. To his left, near the bay beside Olav's hall, the Orkneymen charged along the water, advancing quickly on men who were hastily trying to prepare themselves behind a shabby wooden wall. Erik thought he glimpsed Jarl Sigurd among them, but could not be sure. Ahead of him, on a small rise that led to the base of Mollebakken, a knot of enemy warriors saw Erik's men and scrambled up the hill to the safety of their larger force.

Erik's men climbed the rise in a few strides. To his right, the defenders battled the Danes, though it was a paltry few against an overwhelming onslaught, and they soon broke and retreated up the hill. Every so often a hapless retreater would lose his footing on the muddy slope, slide back into the mass of screaming foe, and die beneath their blades. Along the beach, the men were putting up a stauncher fight behind their makeshift defenses. Erik's main force ran about him, finishing off thralls and women, animals and anything else that stood in their way.

"To me!" His voice tore through the morning like a clap of thunder. "Hordalanders! Fjordmen! To me!" Beside him, his hirdman gave a long blast of his battle horn.

The Northmen finished their slaughter and regrouped around the axe standard of their leader. On the hill, the defenders had reached the crest and were organizing into a defensive line. That, he knew instinctively, was where his brothers would be.

On the right, the Danes did not wait for the signal to attack. Instead, they scrambled after their prey and assaulted the defenses, taking heavy casualties from spears and other projectiles that tore through their ranks. Many of the Danes simply lost their footing on the slick ground and slid, cursing and yelling, down the hill. Others reached the defenders' line, only to be killed or repulsed by the blades of Erik's brothers.

Erik elbowed the man with the horn and pointed his axe at the Danes. "Call them back. We need to attack as one."

The horn sounded and the Danes retreated. On the hill, two banners rose, listless in the rain, but defiant.

Jarl Sigurd had just finished carrying a log from the forest when he heard the shouts. He knew in an instant what was happening and without even turning to look, dropped the log and ran for his gear. His men followed his lead.

"Leave your armor," Sigurd growled at one of his younger hirdmen. "We do not have time."

The trees to the east of the estate seemed to bleed warriors. Hundreds came at his small group, splashing across the beach and through the shallows of the bay. Sigurd rushed for the small rise on which they had built a flimsy defensive barrier — two levels of logs supported by upright stakes. It was not much, but it would at least slow the attackers and give Sigurd and his men something behind which to stand. When he reached it, he raised his sword and yelled, "To me!"

One by one, his Tronds joined him at the wall and faced their enemy. The attackers, more than a hundred men, came on at a full run, screaming their war cries and insults. Sigurd glanced at his men, then back at the enemy, knowing as they came on that he would die this day. And in knowing that, he clenched his jaw, kissed the talisman at his neck, and prepared to meet his fate.

"Shield wall!" he shouted, and his men locked shields in practiced precision.

The enemy slammed into them with a rippling crack so loud, it would have made Thor jealous. Steel pounded on shields. Wood cracked and splintered. Men cried out in pain and frustration and belligerent fury. The Tronds slipped and grunted under the onslaught even as they jammed their own blades into the guts and throats and limbs of their attackers. A speartip knocked Sigurd's helmet askew. He recovered and rammed his blade at a man's shoulder but missed.

More attackers joined the fray. Sigurd staggered as an axe smashed into his shield. The man swung again, missing his mark and falling, off balance. Sigurd drove his sword deep into the warrior's side. Before he could pull the blade free, another man came on. The man sensed Sigurd's peril and brought his sword downward in a powerful two-handed swing. Sigurd met the stroke high with his shield, worked his sword free, and swiped across the man's stomach with his blade. The metal rings burst and the man crumpled to the ground. Another man swung his sword at Sigurd's head, missing narrowly. Sigurd dispatched him with a thrust to the throat.

The foemen fell back to regroup, leaving piles of moaning wounded and wrecked corpses behind. They gathered about their standard, one that Sigurd recognized immediately as that of Orkneymen. He wondered briefly if they belonged to his brother, who long ago had left for the Orkney Islands, then he cast the thought aside — it mattered little now.

"We cannot hold off another attack," called a senior hirdman named Egil. The man had once fought as Harald Fairhair's standard bearer and his advice caused Sigurd to look about. The rank of Tronds had thinned dramatically and he knew instinctively that Egil was right. The Orkneymen would come again, and when they did, they would overwhelm the Tronds. Their position was no longer tenable.

Though he could no longer see what as happening elsewhere, Sigurd could hear the sounds of struggle over on Mollebakken. He hoped that Olav had made it up the hill. He hoped that Sigfrid was still alive. Beside him, Egil swayed on his feet. A gash in his forehead spilled blood over his left eye.

"You are hurt."

"It is a scratch." Egil wiped the blood away. "We cannot stay here."

Sigurd nodded. "Come."

Erik found the Danish leader, Svein, at the base of Mollebakken. He was gathering the remnants of his Danish army while a warrior wrapped a gash in his right forearm.

Svein smacked the man angrily over his head. "Leave it be, you lout! I'll tend to it later."

Erik scanned the hillcrest. "What do you make of their defenses?"

"The defenses are weak and could easily be penetrated, were it not so impossible to stand firmly and fight. Fighting head-on is folly. Mayhap another direction would be easier."

Erik nodded as the Dane confirmed what he already knew. "This is how we shall proceed. Arinbjorn. Come." He motioned to his foster brother. "The plan is as follows. You, Svein, shall attack the north side of the hill, as you have just done. And you, Arinbjorn" — Erik pointed to his white-haired friend — "shall take up position to the south with your Fjordmen. I will attack from here with the remainder."

"But Erik," Svein began to protest, "the ground is —"

Erik silenced him with a glare. "I know well what I am about. Now, Arinbjorn, do not conceal yourselves when flanking the hill. I want our foe to see you moving. When I blow the horn, you, Arinbjorn, will lead off the attack. Svein, wait until you hear the second blast of my horn before attacking. Is that clear?"

The men nodded.

"Good. Now go, and may Odin bring you luck."

Jarl Sigurd's situation was now dire. His men had retreated into the woods behind the rise, taking with them any man able enough to fight. The enemy pursued as soon as the Tronds began their retreat and quickly gained on their prey. It did not take long to realize that Sigurd and his men, many of whom were wounded, would not be able to outrun the Orkneymen. To make matters worse, there was a wide river somewhere before them and fording it would be difficult at best. Tunsberg lay to the north. Sigurd had hoped to find a place in the woods to mount a defense, but there was nowhere to go.

Sigurd ordered a halt and turned. He could see the enemy weaving through the trees, coming ever closer to his men. Around him, his men struggled for breath or wiped at the sweat and blood that mingled with the rainwater on their skin.

"What is the plan?" Egil stood beside him, his chest heaving. The gash on his head continued to flow, albeit not as badly as before.

"Ready yourselves. We are going back," he said.

Erik's men shifted about anxiously, fingering their weapons, checking their armor, their shields, and their helmets. Moments before, he had ordered everyone to remove their boots, hoping traction on the slope would be better with bare feet. Though shivering from the rain, the men obeyed their king.

The attack was going as planned. On the crest of the hill, Erik could see the defenses shifting to meet Arinbjorn's onslaught from the south. At any moment, he would hear the song of battle. Screams. Curses. The crash of wood. The ring of steel. He waited…

There!

"Sound the second horn!" he yelled at his signalman.

The stentorian blast wafted over the landscape, followed instantly by the roar of Danes as they attacked the northern side of the hill. With a wave of his hand Erik called his men to advance, his toes sinking into the cold mud, but holding firm. Behind him, his men moved forward like wraiths, the sound of their approach drowned by the falling rain and the din of battle on the hilltop above.

Halfway there, and still the defenders had not seen them. Two hundred paces. One hundred fifty. One hundred. Fifty.

Someone yelled above them. Erik's men whooped and brandished their weapons at the foe. Through the rain, Erik could see Sigfrid's standard above him, though his brother was invisible behind the shield wall of his towering bodyguards.

"Erik! You witch's spawn! I will kill you myself!" The words came from the cousin of Sigfrid and a loyal member of his hird.

Erik hefted his battle-axe, swinging madly, unaware of the bellow exploding from his throat. The cousin's shield shattered under his blow. The man tried to recover but Erik was already swinging again. The man parried with his sword, but Erik's axe knocked him backward. Before he could regain his footing, the axe blade crushed his helmet and split his skull.

Another man stepped in Erik's way. Erik swung low and cleaved through the warrior's knee. The man fell screaming to the ground and Erik silenced him with a blow to the chest.

The Danes broke through the northern lines, shattering the defenders' left flank. To the south, the defenders held fast against Arinbjorn and his Fjordmen, though order was quickly slipping into chaos. The hilltop was a maelstrom of hacking blades and yells and rain and blood, and Erik laughed, for the battle lust had possessed him and he reveled in it.

Before him, the shield wall of Sigfrid's hird was crumbling, the hapless defenders falling back into battered pockets of desperate men. Erik and his hirdmen pressed into the foe with the bloodthirsty fervor of those who can smell victory. Through the chaos, Erik could see his brother preparing for the final onslaught. His skin was pale, his face a grimace of pain and anger. A blade had sliced through his tunic and blood poured from the opening. Beside him, his standard bearer lay dead on the ground, a spear buried deep in his chest.

"Sigfrid!" Erik's voice carried across the gap that separated them.

Sigfrid was too weak to do anything but turn and look. Erik saw recognition creep into his brother's eyes and watched as it transformed to loathing.

"Lay down your sword," Erik yelled, "and you will be spared!"

There was a moment's hesitation as Sigfrid considered Erik's words. Then, suddenly, he spat a glob of blood from his mouth and smiled. To Erik, it looked almost sad, as if he understood what fate had in store and had resigned himself to it. "I will see you in Valhall, brother." He then lifted his sword and planted his feet.

Around him, the remnants of his bodyguard cheered his bravery and the struggle began anew. Another warrior stepped into Erik's path. Erik brought his axe down toward the man's unprotected head. His opponent saw the move coming and parried the blow high, before it had time to gather momentum. Erik kicked the man between the legs, sending him to his knees, then decapitated him. As the man fell, Erik looked to where his brother had been, but he was gone.

Erik pressed forward and found Sigfrid on the ground, his shield arm smashed, a gaping wound in his chest. Erik forced his way to his brother's side and knelt. Sigfrid's eyes turned slowly to Erik and a distant smile drifted onto his face. "The gods curse you and your reign, brother."

To Erik's left, a mighty cheer rose across the hilltop. Olav, too, had fallen.

Erik stood and turned to his men. "Behead my brothers," he growled to a warrior nearby, "and send their heads to their families. I want all to know what happens to those who defy me."

"We must reach the ships!" Sigurd yelled as the Orkneymen neared. "Stay together and do not stop! If you stop, you die. Onward!" he broke into a run. Behind him, his men joined the cheer.

The shock of seeing the Tronds charging them halted the unorganized Orkneymen in their tracks. Many stood alone with only their shields and their weapons to protect them against this unexpected move. Sigurd sliced through two men before they could even react. A third ducked his blow. Sigurd did not stop to finish him. His legs burned and his lungs stung, but he did not stop to fight.

Ahead of him, a second group of Orkneymen had gathered in a hasty defensive line. A few attempted to throw spears as the Tronds charged them, but the throws were rushed and landed harmlessly. Sigurd lowered his shoulder and barreled into a defender's shield. The man sidestepped at the last moment, his foot tangling with Sigurd's as he did so. Sigurd toppled to the ground, half expecting to feel the burn of the man's blade in his back, but the strike never came. Sigurd scrambled to his feet and ran on.

The shapes of the longships appeared through the trees not more than one hundred paces ahead. A mass of foemen had gathered on the beach near them. They must have heard the fighting in the trees and come to defend the ships. But Sigurd would not be stopped. He would not be killed so close to his ships! Lifting his sword, he let loose a roar of defiance. To his surprise, it was answered by a cacophony of shouts from his Tronds behind him.

With a horrible crash the two lines met on the beach. Defenders toppled backward under the momentum of their assailants. Shields shattered. Bodies crumpled. Weapons hacked and sliced, searching for blood. The Tronds tore into the Orkneymen with every ounce of energy they had left, using whatever weapon was at their disposal: rocks, fists, feet, blades. They fought possessed, for indeed, their survival depended on it.

A group of Tronds broke free and ran for a small knarr, knowing it would be easier to move than the heavy longships. Amidst flying spears, they pushed it into the surf and scrambled aboard, then yelled for their comrades to follow.

More Orkneymen joined the fray. Sigurd cut down another man and prepared for more. At his back, his hirdman Frosti fought two men at once.

"Frosti! We must break from here!"

Frosti swung at an enemy, gaining some room for himself. "I shall not leave until you are safe. Go!"

"Frosti —"

"Go!"

There was no time to argue. Sigurd swung at the foeman facing him, then broke from the engagement. The warrior pursued, but Frosti hacked into the man's back before he could take a step. Four knarrs now rocked in the surf as one by one, the Tronds climbed aboard. Sigurd splashed into the water, then up onto the gunwale of the closest knarr. A pair of hands hauled him into the craft and he collapsed to the deck with a thud.

On the beach, Frosti fought on, his back now to a tree. He swung his sword in great arcs before him, keeping the Orkneymen at a distance. But his arms were weakening, his sword no longer swinging as it had. A man came from his side and drove his spear into Frosti's powerful chest. Still, the mighty Trond managed to retaliate, killing the man with a final desperate swing before he too collapsed to the earth.

More Tronds broke from the battle and climbed aboard the awaiting boats. The enemy pursued them into the water, swinging wildly at the men and the ship. Those already aboard held off the attackers with spears. Quickly the surf filled with Orkneymen and the bodies of those

Tronds not quick enough with their escape. It was no longer safe to stay — they had to go.

"Row!" Sigurd yelled.

The men pulled hard at the oars, gliding away from the deadly beach and out of range of the flying spears. Silhouetted in the flames of Olav's great hall, the last of his Tronds — those who had not made it to the boats — fell under the blades of their enemy. Sigurd watched in feeble rage as one by one they fell.

The North was lost.

Chapter 9

That night, the four knarrs that had escaped Erik's army landed on an island close to the open sea. A hill climbed steadily from the island's beach and disappeared into a thick shroud of low-lying fog, the remnants of the morning's storm. Here and there upon the hill, flat boulders jutted out like tabletops, affording the men scant shelter from the drizzle that continued to fall.

It had been rough rowing for the remnants of the Tronds — twenty-one men in all. The winds remained strong, driving swells relentlessly at their undermanned vessels as they made their way south, away from Tunsberg and the battle. For hours they struggled in the waves that crashed upon their decks and poured into their holds, threatening to sink or capsize each, until at last, as the northern sky dimmed, Sigurd determined it safe enough to put in. Exhausted, most of the men crawled under the rocks and fell immediately into a deep slumber, mindless of the mud and the wetness and the hunger that wracked their bodies.

Beneath one of these boulders, soaked to the bone and shivering, Sigurd sat and listened to the heavy snores of his men. To the north, the coastline faded, like Sigurd's spirits, in the twilight of the approaching night. He could not seem to shake the thought that everything he and his family had done for the past few generations, all the sweat and blood and toil spent on building a small trading empire, amounted, after this day's events, to nothing. What, he wondered, would become of the Trondelag now that Erik had killed Halvdan and Sigfrid? Would old alliances dissolve, or border fights erupt, now that Erik controlled the land? It was hard to know. For certain, Erik would install his own jarls and thanes and would kill or banish all those who opposed his rule, Sigurd being first and foremost among those. This, he surmised sadly, would not be too difficult, since most of those who might oppose Erik had perished in the battle that morning. It was a grim reality and one that made Sigurd sick with heartache.

"May I join you?"

Sigurd peered up at the creased and bloodied face of his hirdman, Egil. Sigurd gestured to the empty space beside him.

Egil sat heavily and wiped the droplets of rain from his bald crown. "So what now?"

Sigurd shrugged. "The way I see it, packing up and moving to Island might be the wisest course."

Egil exhaled in what sounded like a laugh, but may have been disgust.

Sigurd wiped his auburn bangs from his eyes and peered at the aging man. "You do not agree?"

"No. I do not agree."

Sigurd sat for a moment. "Why not?"

Egil sniffed. "Think you for a moment. What is there still in the Trondelag for you?"

The day's events had taken a toll on Sigurd's patience and he spat in response to Egil's question. "I am in no mood for riddles, Egil. I have just lost all that my family has taken generations to build. I have lost friends and comrades and a king. Tell me what is on your mind or leave me in peace."

Egil was not vexed by the sour tone in Sigurd's voice and answered Sigurd calmly. "That is just it. You have lost nothing if you choose not to lose it. You act as if you are a whipped hound, running with your tail between your legs. Today you lost a battle, not your life."

Sigurd's brow puckered. "What do you mean, I have lost nothing? You and I watched as Erik's army cut down the bravest of our warriors. Even if I wanted to, I could not stand against Erik."

"Ah, but you could. All you need is more warriors, and the Trondelag has no shortage of those."

Sigurd sighed, feeling suddenly overwhelmed by Egil's comment. "You are suggesting raising another army?"

Egil turned to him and grinned. "And why not?"

Sigurd stared at his warrior. "Men would not rally to me after this loss. They would need something else to motivate them. Mayhap the support of other fylker." He sighed again. "Halogaland is out — they are far too disunited to offer much help. North and South More?" He shrugged at his own spoken thought. "Jarl Tore might help…"

"You should not discount the Halogalanders. Some might heed your call. What about the Uplands?"

Sigurd grimaced. Over generations, the Uplanders had fought the Tronds time and again for access to Finnmark and the North Sea, both of which the Trondelag blocked by sheer geography. The position allowed the Tronds to control Upland trade to the north and west, and profit on all goods traveling in those directions. "Even if I accepted this plan, the surviving jarls and thanes of the Trondelag would not. There are too many long-standing animosities. I fear that most Tronds would rather accept Erik than an alliance with the Uplanders. Besides, the Uplanders rejected our plea for help here. They are too busy defending themselves against the Swedes, it seems."

"I admit it is a small chance. But what if the call for help came from someone other than a Trond? Someone who could offer them something more? Someone with a rightful claim to Erik's throne? Another of the Yngling line?"

Sigurd was confused. "Perchance the Tronds would follow. But who might that king be? All of Harald's sons are dead, save Erik."

Egil was silent as he let his eyes drift along the gray horizon. When he did speak, his voice came softly. "There is one."

Sigurd wiped the rain from his face as his mind searched for the king to which Egil referred. Suddenly, it struck him. "Of course. Hakon."

Egil flashed a yellow-toothed smile. "Aye."

Sigurd's mind conjured the memory of Hakon being born, for his mother had been en route to meet Harald when the child came and Sigurd had been there to see the child's first cry. Since Harald had not been there, the honor of naming the child fell to Sigurd, who had named him after his own father. Then just as suddenly, the memory vanished. "But he is a boy. He could never —"

"How old were you when you first wielded a sword in battle?"

"Fifteen winters. But he cannot be older than...than twelve or thirteen by now. He is too young. The people would never accept it."

Egil waved his argument aside. "Hakon is fourteen, Sigurd, by my count. I was thirteen when I first went to battle. Harald Fairhair was younger still. And if he is anything like Erik, his eagerness will make up for any lack in physical ability. Besides, think of it. You will be Hakon's advisor, his most trusted councilor. If you succeed, you will have his ear and his trust, and your power will grow. In my eyes, there is no choice but this one. Unless, of course, you want to give up all that your forebears have built."

A thin wisp of a grin creased Sigurd's face as he shook his head. "Odin's arse, Egil. From whence did you dream all this up?"

Egil shrugged. "I have been considering it for some time."

Sigurd nodded thoughtfully. "Suppose I do entertain this idea. It seems to me that there is plenty here yet to plan. For instance, how will we get the jarls to follow this boy king? And if we get past that blockade, how will we convince them to ally with our enemies?"

Egil patted Sigurd's shoulder. "There is yet time to plan and to think. You are a smart man and I know you can come up with something." He scooted from under the boulder and stood. "Give it thought, Sigurd. But do not think over-long. Hakon lives far to the west in Engla-lond. If we are to bring Hakon home, we will need to sail on the morrow to fetch him."

Sigurd crept from under his boulder early the following morning to find that the clouds had broken and the rain had ceased. Despite his having slept little the night before, his spirits were as crisp as the new day and his mood remarkably improved.

After spending much of the previous night in deliberations with himself, and exhausting every thought that came to his mind, Sigurd was convinced that Egil's plan was bold, but possible. It was far from flawless, but it afforded a little hope where, only the night before, none had existed. In addition, it had restored a sense of purpose to Sigurd's life, as well as a modicum of confidence for his future and the future of the realm he and his kin had labored so inexhaustibly to build. Thus heartened, he worked his way down to the beach, where the remainder of his men had already gathered.

He called them together and spoke so that all could hear his words. "Our plans are changing."

He found Egil's face in the crowd. "The remaining members of my hird will take three of the four ships and sail for Engla-lond. There you will seek out King Athelstan and bring his charge, Hakon Haraldsson, back to my estate at Lade. I am placing Egil in charge, so heed his word. The remaining five of you will sail with me back to Lade, where we will make plans for our defense against Erik."

"What of supplies?" called one of the hirdmen. "Engla-lond is a long way away and we have no food or change of clothing."

Sigurd silenced him with a lifted hand. "You are all resourceful and I trust that you will not starve. There are many farms along the coastline, as well as fishing nets in the boats. As for clothes, I believe you will find those in the same place you will find the food. Do whatever it takes to bring the boy back to Lade. Are there any questions?"

The men looked at each other, but not a man spoke.

"Good. Then Odin willing, I will see you all when you have returned from Athelstan's kingdom. Make haste. We have no time to spare."

The men scrambled to arrange themselves in their ships. As they did, Egil pulled Sigurd aside. "What should we do with the boy if Erik kills you before our return?"

Sigurd deliberated on that gloomy reality before speaking. "What was it you said to me last night? Ah, yes." He patted Egil on the shoulder. "You are a smart man and I know you can come up with something." He smiled, then sobered. "Three winters ago, you came to me for a reason, Egil. You did not support Erik. If I die before you return, see this through. Support the boy and rid this land of Erik."

Egil grinned. "Farewell. I will see you again before the leaves start to turn."

Sigurd watched him walk away. "May Odin bring you luck, Egil."

Erik climbed through the wreckage of bodies to the top of Mollebakken. The corpses had been stripped of their weapons and their wealth and left to the ravens and seagulls that now gorged on their flesh. At the crest of the hill, he turned and peered southward, down the waterway through which Jarl Sigurd and some of his men had escaped. He had thought to pursue them, but his men had been busy stripping the dead and celebrating their hard-won victory. To organize a pursuit would have been like prying red meat from a wolf's jaws. Besides, Jarl Sigurd was a defeated man — Erik would find him soon enough and cut him down along with the remainder of those whoreson Tronds.

He turned his gray-green eyes to the clearing sky and smiled. The mighty oak of Harald had fallen and the Norns had seen his fate come to pass. He and his army of hounds had prevailed.

There was nothing and no one standing in his way now.

Dear reader,

We hope you enjoyed reading *Mollebakken*. Please take a moment to leave a review, even if it's a short one. Your opinion is important to us.

Discover more books by Eric Schumacher at https://www.nextchapter.pub/authors/eric-schumacher-historical-fiction-author.

Want to know when one of our books is free or discounted? Join the newsletter at http://eepurl.com/bqqB3H.

Best regards,
Eric Schumacher and the Next Chapter Team

You might also like:
God's Hammer by Eric Schumacher

To read the first chapter for free, please head to: https://www.nextchapter.pub/books/gods-hammer-historical-viking-adventure

Historical Notes

As I said in my Foreword, I feel the battle of Mollebakken is one of the more critical battles of the Viking Age. Though Harald Fairhair had already abdicated his High Seat to his favorite son, Erik Bloodaxe, Erik's half-brothers rejected him as king. Had Erik failed to defeat his half-brothers at Mollebakken, or had he been killed at Mollebakken, the history of Norway and Northern England (where Erik would eventually rule) would have been completely altered.

There are several other elements in this story that bear some explanation.

First, the proper spelling of King Sigfrid's name is Sigrød. I changed it to ease pronunciation.

Second, there is the matter of Erik's wife, Gunnhild. Most authors and historians believe Gunnhild to be the daughter of Gorm the Old of Denmark and sister to Harald Bluetooth. Given the long history of strife between the peoples of Viking Age Norway and Denmark, as well as their equal thirst for expansion, it would make sense on a number of levels for the Norwegian prince to marry a Danish princess. It would also explain why, after Erik's eventual death, King Harald Bluetooth of Denmark supported Gunnhild and her sons. *Heimskringla* tells a different tale. In that telling, Erik found Gunnhild in a hut in Finnmark and believed her to be the most beautiful woman he had ever seen. Her father was said to be Ozur Toti from Halogaland, and that she came to Finnmark to learn sorcery from two Finns who were known to be skilled in the craft. This is probably the less accurate of the two tales, but it was the more intriguing and played into the storyline.

Ragnvald is the name of Erik's oldest son. In this tale, I show him alive, though at some point in his youth (as it is stated in *Egil's Saga*, which chronicles the life of the Norse outlaw and Viking, Egil Skallagrimsson), Ragnvald is killed by Egil.

Tønsberg (Old Norse, *Túnsberg*, or Tunsberg as I have spelled it in this book) is often regarded as one of the oldest towns in Viking Age Norway, though some argue that Kaupang farther south came first. The town's name originally referred to the fortification on a "mountain" known as Castle Mountain, or Slottsfjellet. Why the army of Olav and Sigfrid would abandon the fortification to fight Erik on a different hill farther to the east is unknown. There is no indication that it was called Mollebakken (Old Norse: Møllebakken, which means Mill Hill) back then. However, I wanted to give the place a name.

In addition, nothing is known of the actual battle save that we believe Erik had the larger army, that he was victorious, and that both Olav and Sigfrid fell. We do not know if he had help from the Orkneys or Denmark. We also do not know if Jarl Sigurd was there, though it is plausible that he was part of King Sigfrid's host.

Finally, Harald Fairhair's death is usually placed around AD 932–934. I split the difference and placed it in AD 933, the same year in which the battle at Mollebakken is said to have taken place.

Other Books by Eric Schumacher

If you are curious about who ultimately rules the North, whether Gunnhild's premonition comes to pass, or whether Jarl Sigurd's ploy to find Hakon succeeds, pick up the trilogy *Hakon's Saga* from Amazon or Audible and find out.

Book 1 – *God's Hammer*
Book 2 – *Raven's Feast*
Book 3 – *War King*

About the Author

Eric Schumacher was born in Los Angeles in 1968. He is the author of three historical fiction novels — *God's Hammer, Raven's Feast,* and *War King* — and one novella. All tell the story of the first Christian king of Viking Norway, Hakon Haraldsson, and his struggles to gain and hold the High Seat of his realm.

Schumacher's fascination with Vikings and medieval history began at a young age, though exactly why is not clear. While Los Angeles has its own unique history, there are no destroyed monasteries or Viking burial sites or hidden hoards buried in fields. Still, from the earliest age, he was drawn to books about medieval kings and warlords and was fascinated by their stories and the turbulent times in which they lived. He is also certain that Tolkien helped feed his imagination with his Norse-infused stories of Middle Earth.

Schumacher now resides in Santa Barbara with his wife and two children, and is busy working on his next book.

He can be found here:
Website: ericschumacher.net
Facebook: www.facebook.com/EricSchumacherAuthor
Twitter: @DarkAgeScribe

Mollebakken
ISBN: 978-4-86750-043-9 (Large Print)

Published by
Next Chapter
1-60-20 Minami-Otsuka
170-0005 Toshima-Ku, Tokyo
+818035793528
3rd June 2021

www.ingramcontent.com/pod-product-compliance
Lightning Source LLC
LaVergne TN
LVHW092012090526
838202LV00002B/112